Redwood

AND OTHER POEMS

By
ADLAI ALBERT ESTEB, B.TH., M.A., Ph.D.

Author of *Driftwood, Sandalwood, Kindle Kindness, Rosewood, Firewood, Scrapwood,* and *Morning Manna*

11938

REVIEW AND HERALD PUBLISHING ASSOCIATION
WASHINGTON, D.C.

Introduction

Some anonymous seer has said that a horizon is but the limit of our sight. And to that thought might be added a new beatitude: Blessed is the man who pushes out the horizons for his generation.

Hazlitt, the brilliant essayist, tells us that when he was a young lad his mind was listless and his faculties unawakened. Then it happened one day that the poet Coleridge came to visit his father, and that evening young Hazlitt accompanied the visitor for several miles on his homeward journey. In one of his later essays he tells what that walk meant to him. For the first time he was the companion of one who dealt in "horizons" and who opened the doors of magic realms of thought and vision.

It is the scintillating verse of our beloved Adlai Albert Esteb—poet, orator, and minister—that brings that story back with refreshing recurrence. The profound spiritual depth of his ministry and all the power of his oratory underlie the magnificence of Dr. Esteb's poetic works. In all his previous volumes, and again now in *Redwood,* he has succeeded so admirably and immensely in pushing out the horizons for his fellow men.

Art is beauty in conception and expression; architecture is beauty in proportion; culture is beauty in mind and manner; grace is beauty in motion; eloquence is beauty in speech, and may we not add that a perfect tree, such as *Sequoia sempervirens* in all its stately grandeur, is the quintessence of beauty in nature. It was Charles Kingsley who wrote that "beauty is God's handwriting." Welcome it therefore in every fair face, every fair sky, every fair flower, and now in every fair line of Adlai Albert Esteb's *Redwood.*

CONGRESSMAN JERRY L. PETTIS
Thirty-third District, California

Dr. and Mrs. Adlai A. Esteb, with Congressman Jerry L. Pettis, of California, in front of Capitol.

Congressional Record

United States of America

PROCEEDINGS AND DEBATES OF THE 91st CONGRESS, SECOND SESSION

Vol. 116   WASHINGTON, TUESDAY, FEBRUARY 3, 1970   *No. 13*

House of Representatives

THE LINCOLN MEMORIAL

(Mr. PETTIS asked and was given permission to address the House for 1 minute, to revise and extend his remarks and include extraneous material.)

Mr. PETTIS. Mr. Speaker, in a few days we will be paying tribute to that great American, Abraham Lincoln, on the occasion of his birthday. It is my purpose today to read a poem written about this great American and the monument to him in this city which we all know.

This poem is written by the poet laureate of the Seventh-Day Adventist Church, Adlai Esteb.

The poem follows:

THE LINCOLN MEMORIAL
(By Dr. Adlai Albert Esteb)

What do we see in Lincoln's form and face?
Mere marble loveliness and sculptured grace?
Much more! We see a poem carved in stone;
We see a moral giant on a throne;
We see, some think, the greatest spot on
    earth,
For here each human being grows in worth.
We see a champion of true liberty,
Emancipator, Man of Destiny!
What inspiration ev'ry look imparts,
And kindles Freedom's flame within our
    hearts!

What do we hear while in this sacred place?
Just whispered plaudits by the human race?
Much more! Methinks I hear a trumpet blast,
A stirring, ringing challenge from the past.
This great incarnate conscience of our land,
Spoke in a voice all men could understand.
His warning words which rang with earnest
    tone,
Now echo through this monument of stone.
"The great unfinished task," he seems to say,
"Demands our dedication here today."

What do we feel mid sculptured art so fine?
Just passing pride in this great national
    shrine?
Far more! We feel the heart throbs of our
    race,
While looking up at Lincoln's furrowed face.
A deep conviction stirs within our souls,
A burning zeal to reach life's highest goals.
We feel, while standing in this place sublime,
Inspired to grasp our heritage of time!
Thank God for Lincoln's call to great and
    small,
Of liberty and justice for us all.

Facsimile of the *Congressional Record* showing poem on Lincoln Memorial read by Pettis on floor of House.

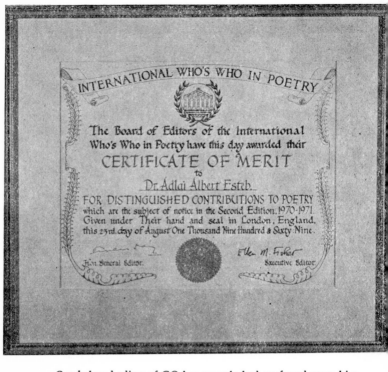

Our beloved editor of GO has recently had conferred upon him the Certificate of Merit by *International Who's Who in Poetry*. It was awarded for his distinguished contributions to poetry.

I am sure there are few of our church members who do not know Elder A. A. Esteb by his poetry, even though they may never have had the opportunity to meet him. The rhythmic lines that seem to flow from his pen have appeared in many of our publications, and he has just finished his sixth volume of poetry, entitled *Redwood*.

Congratulations, Brother Esteb. We look forward to reading many more of your lovely poems in the future. The honor that has been given to you is richly deserved.

ROBERT H. PIERSON
President, General Conference
of Seventh-day Adventists

Redwood

One summer day, long years ago,
Beneath the sunshine's sparkling glow,
We walked along a mountain stream
(My favorite place to rest and dream)
And close beside our mountain trail,
A wondrous, rustic fence of rail.
That fence, built by the pioneers,
Had stood the storms of many years.
"Why is this fence still strong and good?"
I asked my guide. He said, "Redwood."
"But what's the diff'rence?" I replied,
And then you should have seen my guide.
He turned and looked at me and said,
With voice that showed concern and dread,
"Come, sit down, son, and rest awhile.
Before we go another mile
There is a story you must hear
About an early pioneer
Who thought that woods were all the same;

He had not heard of redwood's fame.
He learned the hard way, I would say,
And what a price he had to pay—
His wife, his home, one little boy,
A life devoid of hope and joy.
I hesitate to tell the tale,
And I'll not tell you each detail,
But I must tell enough to show
The lesson you will need to know,
For you might make the same mistake,
And bring yourself the same heartache.
For you are young, too young yourself
To throw away your life for pelf!

"Well, here's the story you should hear
About this early pioneer.
He came out West while very young,
With healthy body, heart, and lung.
He seemed to have no fear of sin,
His motto was 'Don't fence me in.'
He left his home, I'm sure you see,
Because *he wanted to be 'free.'*
Well, 'free' he was, and spent his youth,
And drowned convictions of the truth,
For he would show that he could go
His own sweet way and none would know.
For years he showed no real concern—
He never even cared to learn—
About *'the good, the better, best,'*
And nothing had to stand a test.
He would not hear a warning voice,
Or be selective in his choice.
With bluff and snuff he acted tough,

Said, 'Anything is good enough.'
With this philosophy of life,
He built his house and took a wife;
He ate his food, he drank his drink;
What words he'd speak, what thoughts he'd think.
Where he would go, what books he'd buy,
To tell the truth or tell a lie—
He really did not seem to care
What he would say or what he'd wear.
How he would live or what he'd do—
He did not care to know your view.
He had no sense of right or wrong—
Went with the crowd that sang this song:
'It makes no diff'rence what one does.'
He did not know how wrong he was!
'Twas years before he came to know
We reap in life just what we sow!
The best in life is none too good—
For this great truth he'd thank redwood!
Too late he learned this vital truth,
But by that time he'd lost his youth.
Ah, then he'd sit here by this stream,
Although he seemed too old to dream,
But dream he did—his dreams were good.
He'd teach the world about redwood!
With deep remorse about his past,
He came to see himself at last;
Now he would try and make amends
For all his life's lost dividends.
He'd build a rail fence by this stream
Where passers-by might pause and dream.
And view his termite-ridden house
(The place he lost his child and spouse)

Comparing it with this rail fence,
Built with such care and diligence.
The house he built with cheaper brand,
The fence with finest in the land."

The old guide paused and glanced at me,
Then looked again as if to see
If what he'd said had reached my heart.
If so, he had more to impart.
I sat spellbound, I was all ears
(I hoped he hadn't seen my tears).
I asked my guide, "Before we go
There's more that I would like to know.
How did he lose his wife and boy?
What was it robbed him of his joy?"
That dear old guide, with snow-white hair,
Was pleased that someone seemed to care,
He looked at me with tear-dimmed eyes,
And then I had a great surprise.
He said, while brushing off a tear,
"Young man, I was that pioneer!
I built my life on sin and crime,
Instead of making it sublime.
I built my home with poor-rate stuff,
And thought it all was good enough.
For floors I did not use redwood;
The wood I used was just no good,
And termites soon began to work,
While all my duties I would shirk.
I went to town to find a wife
To help me live my rugged life.
Again I made the same mistake
And got a girl who brought heartache.

I really had not thought before,
If best wives come from wild dance floor?
And *yet we tried* to make a home,
A place from which we need not roam.
In time a darling boy and girl
Soon kept our household in a whirl.

"Then we began to reap with tears,
The harvest of my wasted years.
While I was in the field one day,
And stacking up our crop of hay,
I heard a scream come from the house,
And I was sure it was my spouse.
I ran back home, what did I find?
I found my attitude of mind
Had laid a rotten floor—that's true,
And my own wife had fallen through.
I pulled her out, she was so frail,
With her right leg gashed by a nail.
We washed away the bloodied clot;
I thought she'd need a tetanus shot,
But since she said, 'I'm better now,'
I didn't carry out my vow.
I took the easy road again—
A trait too common with all men.
My wife grew worse, her fever high,
We sent for help, for fear she'd die.
But when the doctor came at last,
Too late it was to shrive my past.
So my philosophy of life
Had cost me now my pretty wife.
In my poor way I tried, in fact,
To keep the family all intact.

"When Jack was ten he hounded me
To build a playhouse in a tree.
But I was busy, and it's true
I didn't know just what to do.
Day after day he'd come and say,
'Let's build our playhouse, Dad, today.'
I'd look into that cherub face—
But gave my own boy second place.
One day he started all alone
To build his playhouse on his own.
That day he climbed up in that tree;
When I came home—what did I see?
My boy had fallen from a limb
And broken his neck, there I found him.
I'd killed my boy but not with swords—
I'd let him build with rotten boards.
I'd missed my golden chance to show
My boy how he should build and grow.
I'd killed my boy, I'd killed my wife,
With my philosophy of life.
I stood there stunned, I raised my eyes,
And cried, 'O God, You rule the skies.
Forgive me for my wicked deeds,
And look upon my heartfelt needs,
And from this day help me discern
The lessons I've refused to learn.
God, *You* must have a better plan
For me. Make me a diff'rent man!'

"From that day, son, God took control
And helped me see life's highest goal.
Within the clutch of circumstance,
I thanked God for that one more chance!

My new philosophy of life
Could not bring back my boy or wife,
But it could help my darling girl
Become the Master's precious pearl.
I'd build a life and home on earth,
To teach of things of greatest worth.
God helped me build for little Jean
A home of happiness serene.
We had our worships every day
And from the Bible learned God's way.
And when Jean went away to school
I *knew* she'd keep the golden rule!
With her philosophy of life
She soon became a preacher's wife.
My heart was full of hope and pride!
Then I became a mountain guide;
I too would guide man's wayward feet
To walk at last God's golden street.
God has restored each wasted year
Of that rebellious pioneer."

The old guide paused, a smile of grace
Then lighted up his radiant face.
I stood and grasped his hands in mine,
And looked long in his face benign.
I stood there speechless for a while;
Then through my tears I tried to smile.
I saw a rainbow through my tears;
It gave me hope and banished fears.
I said, while gaining self-control,
"Your story deeply moves my soul.
My mind and heart are truly stirred,
It's been the greatest tale I've heard.

I'm just a lad, a teen-age boy;
Your story fills my heart with joy.
I've made decisions here today—
I want to walk God's grand highway;
I also want to be God's guide.
I vow I'll choose a Christian bride
To help me build a home of worth—
A little bit of heav'n on earth.

"I thank you, Sir, for what you've done,
For now my life's work has begun.
To young and old I'll plead, 'Be good,
And heed the story of redwood!'"

EPILOGUE

Now, after fifty years of time,
I thank God for His work sublime!
I thank Him for the pioneers—
We reap the harvest of their years.
I think of Enoch's marvelous life,
Triumphant in all earthly strife.
Before translation he pleased God.
So, pleasing God, let's onward plod.
In *all* decisions hear God's voice;
With each right choice you can rejoice.
So choose the best, the right, the good—
Be strong, live long, just like redwood!

SECTION 1

To the Seven Churches

What the Spirit Is Saying

1. TO THE INDIFFERENT CHURCH—
To Ephesus and all churches like her,
"REPENT."
See Revelation 2:1-7

To the churches the Spirit is speaking:
I know what your members are seeking!
   "Repent," for your "first love" is "lost,"
At, oh, what a frightening cost!

What is there on earth
Of sufficient worth

To lure us away
From the work of the day,
Till we forget to pray?

With the world on fire,
What does God require?

The Spirit is saying, "Repent"
Before your lifetime is spent.
Repent for your sins of commission;
Repent for your sins of omission.
Repent for time's challenge unheeded.
Repent for your progress impeded.
Repent and—while you are praying—
Hear what the Spirit is saying:

"REPENT."

What the Spirit Is Saying

2. TO THE NEGLECTFUL CHURCH—

To Smyrna and all churches like her,
REALIZE YOUR RICHES.
See Revelation 2:8-11

To the churches the Spirit is speaking,
My treasures are not what you're seeking!
Realize your riches, for you are not poor.
I've boundless resources to help you endure.

I'm speaking to you,
There's much yet to do!

In this moral night
Stand firm for the right,
And turn on the light!

Fear not your fleeting breath,
Be faithful until death,

And I, the Spirit, will give you *a crown*.
Eternal treasures, eternal renown.
They're yours! No longer say you are poor;
I'll give you true riches—your future is sure!
Be faithful in service, be faithful in prayer,
Be faithful in trials, on Me cast all care.
Be faithful! To keep you from straying—
Hear what the Spirit is saying:

    REALIZE YOUR RICHES.

What the Spirit Is Saying

3. TO THE OVERTOLERANT CHURCH—
To Pergamos and all churches like her,
    HOLD FAST.
    See Revelation 2:12-17

To the churches the Spirit has spoken,
To the members with promises broken.
    I know where you live, I know what you do.
    I have a few matters to bring against you.

2

You tolerate sin,
Without and within;

And this, too, I ken,
You tolerate men,
Who, time and again,

Foster false teaching,
Engage in false preaching.

And yet you are trying to hold to My cause,
And have not denied My faith or My laws.
Hold fast and my hidden manna you'll eat;
Hold fast, and your vict'ry will yet be complete.
Hold fast, and I'll give you a precious white stone,
Along with a name that will be all your own.
Hold fast, and great blessings on you I'll convey,
    So hear what the Spirit is saying, today:

        HOLD FAST.

What the Spirit Is Saying

4. TO THE COMPROMISING CHURCH—

To Thyatira and all churches like her,
        DON'T COMPROMISE.
        See Revelation 2:18-29

To the churches the Spirit is talking,
And questions with whom you are walking!
    Is it the Master, whose eyes flame like fire,
    Who knows all your ways and every desire?

Do you compromise
And rationalize

About what's right and wrong?
What is this siren song,
That sinning makes you strong?

These are but Satan's lies!
With truth don't temporize!

But you have compromized with Jezebel,
Who lures to dance above trap doors of hell;
Claims "situation ethics" sets you "free,"
And open sin is "new morality."
Don't compromise with sin and lose your soul;
Be true to God as needle to the pole!
Don't compromise! Instead, take time to pray,
And hear the Spirit speaking ev'ry day:
DON'T COMPROMISE!

What the Spirit Is Saying

5. TO THE LIFELESS CHURCH—
To Sardis and all churches like her,
"BE WATCHFUL."
See Revelation 3:1-6

To Sardis the Spirit has said,
You're *loveless* and *lifeless* and *dead!*
I say, to your sorrow and shame,
You're a church with only a name.

"Be watchful," I pray,
And hear Me today,

And strengthen each thing
Which remains for the King,
If song of the victor you'd sing!

If not, I cannot lie,
Those things are soon to die!

BEWARE of *nominal Christianity!*
The antidote: the mind of Christ in thee!
Be watchful in study, watchful in prayer;
Be watchful in service, good news to share!
Be watchful while meeting earth's woes and strife—
Lest I blot thy name from the book of life!
Be watchful! To keep you safe from straying,
Hear what the Spirit of Christ is saying:

"BE WATCHFUL!"

What the Spirit Is Saying

6. TO THE CHURCH OF OPPORTUNITY—
To Philadelphia and all churches like her,
LET NO ONE TAKE YOUR CROWN!
See Revelation 3:7-13

To the churches the Spirit would speak,
For He who is wise, pure, and meek,
Can solve the myst'ries with which earth is rife,
For He holds the keys to the problems of life.

I told you before,
I tell you once more,

    A door opens wide,
    With chances untried,
    But I'll be your guide.

I pledge you My word;
I hope it is heard.

I plead with you, Let no one take your crown!
I know what you have done throughout your town.
Because you've kept My Word, obeyed My call,
I'll keep you when My final judgments fall.
I'm coming soon, I'm coming back to earth;
Hold fast to what you have of greatest worth.
So grasp your opportunities with zeal,
And hear the Spirit making His appeal:

    LET NO ONE TAKE YOUR CROWN!

What the Spirit Is Saying

7. TO THE COMPLACENT CHURCH—

To Laodicea and all churches like her,
    "BE ZEALOUS."
    See Revelation 3:14-22

To the churches the Spirit is pleading,
With our Father's great *love* interceding,
    You are "lukewarm," not hot or cold;
    I beg of you, "buy of me gold!"

I stand at your door,
As I have oft before,

And here's what I find:
You're wretched and blind,
Complacent, unkind!

You must now relent,
You must now repent!

"Be zealous"! With eyesalve anoint your blind eyes,
And get a new look at your heav'nly prize.
You say, "I am rich," but you're so poor, I vow,
So shake off conceit and complacency *now!*
I will spue you out of my mouth *unless*
You wear the white robe of My righteousness.
Open your door, and I'll come in to stay—
Hear what the Spirit doth urgently say:

"Be Zealous"!

Redemptive Themes

Mountain Peaks of Redemption

Come look at four great truths, grand mountain peaks,
  Involved in your redemption and in mine.
Each one helps tell the story and each speaks
  In eloquence of God's great love divine.

THE FIRST COMING OF CHRIST
"Unto us a child is born"

Since Christ was born "in the fullness of time,"
  It's clear, 'twas part of a purposeful plan;
"For God so loved the world" with love sublime,
  He gave His Son to seek and save lost man!

O come behold this pure, majestic gem,
  This matchless Pearl of Greatest Price, indeed;
The infinite myst'ries of Bethlehem,
  Where Christ, as babe, was born to meet man's need!

"To you this day, good news," the shepherds heard
  The angel choir—how sweetly did they sing.
This mountain peak of love proclaims the word
  Made flesh—the Babe, the newborn King!

THE DEATH OF CHRIST ON THE CROSS

But come, behold a second mountain peak,
  And see your Lord and King on Calv'ry's cross.
Now listen to your Saviour's dying shriek—
  'Twas thus He drank sin's cup of dregs and dross!

He paid the price of sin for man, in fact!
  I ask, Has love e'er reached such depths or heights?
By this vicarious deed—time's greatest act—
  Eternal life was pledged, but what dark nights!

THE RESURRECTION OF CHRIST

Now catch a gleam of glory in the gloom
   And hear the thrilling message He will give,
As Christ our living Lord steps from the tomb
   And shouts, *"Because I live ye too shall live!"*

Here is the proof of everlasting life;
   Here is the promise we will never die;
Here is our comfort in all earthly strife;
   Here is the hope of our home in the sky!

THE SECOND COMING OF CHRIST

Now come and see a fourth transcendent scene,
   As Christ returns to earth a conquering king,
To take us to that heav'nly home serene,
   To join the angels in the songs they sing!

The dead in Christ will hear the Victor's voice,
   And they will then come forth from dusty graves;
The living saints behold Him and rejoice
   And shout with utter joy that Jesus saves!

Since Christ the Son of God a babe was born,
   Since cruel nails once pierced His hands and feet,
This Christ who rose from death will come one morn,
   And our redemption *then* will be complete!

These mighty truths in God's divine design
   Provide redemptive power to save our race!
These mountain peaks of love should ever shine,
   Reflected in each Christian's radiant face!

The Night Was Made for Dreams

The night was made for dreams,
Because in noisy day, it seems,
Earth's vain distractions lure our eyes
Away from visions in the skies.

But, turn off artificial light—
Then glories gleam throughout the night!
In silent nights you see afar
And gaze upon some shining star.

Its quiet peace, of priceless worth,
Contrasts with noise and wars of earth.
This calmness penetrates your soul—
You're *now* earth's pris'ner on parole!

You now are free to break the chains
That bind you to financial gains.
You feel an ecstasy that sings
Of freedom from material things!

This precious truth becomes your own:
"Man cannot live by bread alone!"
You contemplate such holy themes,
And know that night was made for dreams!

Harmony at Last

Behold the wonders of redeeming love,
    The thrill and rapture of that blessed hour
When, in our Father's perfect home above,
    We're saved at last by His almighty power.

Earth's wars of strife have ended,
    And 'tis plain, no more will hate and discord mar earth's
        sod;
Peace, pure and sweet and splendid,
    Then shall reign, with man once more in harmony with
        God.

Feeding on the Word

"He who opens the Scriptures, and feeds upon the heavenly manna, becomes a partaker of the divine nature."—ELLEN G. WHITE, in *Review and Herald*, June 28, 1892.

When op'ning up the sacred Word,
    It's not enough to *read;*
The second step comes when you're stirred,
    And when your soul you *feed.*

The Morning Manna is so sweet,
    When you digest each line,
Partaking thus of life complete—
    God's nature so divine!

Life's Uncertainties

When you say you're healthy, wealthy, and well,
    You naturally want to remain that way;
But mankind is dancing o'er trap doors of hell,
    And we could lose all in a single day.

For life is uncertain, as all of us know,
    And what can one do when his heartbeats cease?
Are we ready now for death's final blow?
    Would we meet our Maker and God in peace?

"I am the way, the truth, and the life,"
  So said the Master to me in my youth;
And I've been sustained mid earth's stress and strife,
  By walking His *way* and teaching His *truth,*

And living His *life*—this secret I share:
When He reigns within we are safe anywhere!

The Blessed Resurrection

O happy day when Christ will come
  And call each sleeping saint;
Of joys the sum, millennium
      That day will start!
      Who has the art,
That glorious scene to paint?

At last from ev'ry dusty grave
  The dead in Christ will rise;
He who forgave now comes to save!
      With lusty voice
      They will rejoice
And meet Him in the skies!

The living saints with rapture stand,
  So happy and serene;
In ev'ry land, with upraised hand,
      The young and old
      With joy behold
That transcendental scene!

This was the blessed hope of man
  In all the ages past;

Since time began this was God's plan,
    To save the lost,
    At any cost.
That hour has come at last!

"I know," said Job, with faith sublime,
  "That my redeemer lives."
Mid trumpet chime, in that last time,
    He'll cause my sod
    To see my God!
Eternal life He gives!

The resurrection of the dead—
  A Christian doctrine pure.
Christ has, we've read, the keys, He said,
    To ev'ry grave,
    And He will save
The sleeping saints for sure!

O let us bring mankind this hope;
  The world is full of strife.
With grief men grope, with problems cope—
    Sin is the first,
    Death is the worst,
But Christ can give us life!

Inspiration

Our minds were stirred
  By what we heard.
Our souls were fed
  With living bread!

Hope an Anchor

Ah! Hope is to the Christian what anchor is to ship;
And every vessel trav'ling on a near or distant trip
Depends so much on anchors in the storms with which
       they cope.
At times not crew or compass, but the anchor, gives them
       hope.
And so it is with Christians in the heavy storms of earth,
When all else fails we still have hope, God's gift of
       priceless worth!

Christ Is Coming for People

Since Christ is coming to earth again,
He wants to redeem the race of men.
He's not coming back for church or steeple,
But coming again to save His people.

It's not the hospitals, or size of our schools,
How large our presses, how sharp our tools,
Or merely how clever our tongue or pen
That guarantees Christ will soon come again.

The Spirit of God is our direst need;
For this great gift we must daily plead,
For only thus can God's work be done,
And our tasks be finished at set of sun.

Then Christ will return to save His own,
And take us home to our Father's throne.
He's coming for people, not houses or land,
He's taking His people to glory land.

Religion in Practice

Do We Really Care?

We sent our workers overseas
  And promised them our full support;
While they faced darkness and disease,
  The years for them grew long, not short.

How often to them do we write?
   Do we know *here* how they are *there?*
How can our conscience feel all right
   Without the proof we really care?

Let's practice love, 'tis our belief,
   And write more letters "over there."
'Twill give our conscience sweet relief
   And prove to them we really care!

Purpose

"Daniel purposed in his heart . . ." Dan. 1:8.
"I am going there on purpose to prepare a place for you." John 14:3, N.E.B. *

A man without a purpose, living on this earth,
Is like a ship with rudder lost—of very little worth.
A man who has a purpose, sure and firm and true,
Reveals the Spirit's power in what he has to do.
A man who has a purpose has *more* than mere desire,
Wherever he may journey, he carries living fire.
His faith will melt the icebergs of indifference and fear,
Dispelling doubts, he then can generate real cheer.
A man without a purpose has let slip from his own soul
The one ingredient needed to help him reach life's goal.

Commitment

A Christian needs a mission,
   For aimlessness is worse
For men without a vision
   Than any other curse.

"His Thing"

The devil flees in full dismay
To see a man kneel down to pray,
For Satan knows a happy saint,
Who never frowns, will never faint!
Ah! Here's a living Christian "ad"—
The finest that the church has had,
The greatest picture man can paint,
When one lives life with due restraint;
Keeps clean in body, mind, and soul
And every day shows self-control.
He shuns the passing fads of man,
Accepts, instead, the Christian plan
Of modesty and virtuous life,
And has no part in sinful strife.
He's not ashamed to be called "quaint";
He triumphs over each complaint.
He does not cling to worldly things,
You'll know him by the songs he sings.
He runs life's race, each patient mile;
The love of God shines through his smile.
He cherishes a worthy goal—
His list of souls on Heaven's scroll!
A man so brave, so true, so pure,
Will do a work that will endure.
On earth he walks, a moral king!
'Tis *thus* a Christian does "his thing."

Modern Morons

To believe in heaven
    and not prepare—
This is the way a moron would care.

To believe in health
   but refuse to eat—
This is folly that can't be beat.

To believe in harvests
   but refuse to sow—
This is the stupidest thing I know!

On Solving Problems

Every day we face our problems,
   But we dare not run away;
For the wrestling with our problems
   Strengthens us to win the day!

Every morning brings fresh problems,
   But this lesson we well know,
The solving of these problems
   Helps the church of God to grow!

The Power of *The Signs*

In World War I we sent *The Signs*
   To Brother Lem, "Somewhere in France";
They never reached him at "front lines"—
   At last, when shot, he had his chance.

They rushed him to a rear base post,
   Away from all the frenzied strife.
While there, what was it helped him most?
   The Signs and medics saved his life!

Not just his earthly life was spared,
   Eternal life was brought to view;

And all because his loved ones *cared*—
   That's what all Christians ought to do.

While he was convalescing there,
   The Signs helped him to pass the time.
But soon he saw a vision rare—
   God's Book revealed its truth sublime.

At first *The Signs* made him so mad
   He threw the magazine away;
But when retrieved it made him glad—
   A nurse came by and saved the day.

She saw a sight of gloom and doom,
   And asked, "What can I do for thee?"
"I threw a *Signs* across the room,
   Please will you bring it back to me?"

She found the magazine and said,
   "Is this the *Signs* you threw away?"
He answered "Yes, the things I read
   Have stirred and haunted me all day!"

You see the *Signs* has mighty power,
   It does not argue with a man,
But simply tells the truth each hour,
   And that's the genius of the plan.

'Twas thus my brother in his youth
   Received the truth that conquers fears.
He gave his life to preach that truth,
   And preached that truth for forty years!

The Call of the Hour

We've heard the call for revival,
   It rings in our ears day and night.
Man's only hope for survival—
   Prepare for the triumph of right.

This reformation is pressing,
   In view of the shortness of time.
The world's great need, so distressing,
   Demands our response be sublime.

Revival and reformation—
   Impressive preludes to power;
They bring the grand consummation!
   Ah! *They* meet the need of the hour!

This vision thrills our hearts and eyes,
   Truth's banner *now* will be unfurl'd.
This challenge comes—Evangelize!
   Evangelize in all the world!

"The Want of the World"

"The want of the world is the want of men,"
Men who are noble and humble and true.
The need of the hour is the need of men,
Men who are faithful in all that they do.

   Men who cannot be bought or sold,
   Men immune from the lure of gold.

Men who will heed time's urgent call
And stand for right though the heavens fall!

As true to truth as needle to pole,
Without a price tag on their soul!

The Human Touch

Shun Stylites' seat—he carried no load,
  Sitting above the crowd so high.
Come down and live by the side of the road
  With helping hands for passers-by.

In giving the gospel there's no better plan
Than getting in touch with our fellow man.

Knowledge and Power for This Crisis Hour
(The Motto for the Laymen's Congress)

"We preach Christ crucified," the *dunamis* of God and the *sophia*
of God (1 Cor. 1:23, 24. We have supplied the Greek words
dunamis and *sophia* for "power" and "wisdom." We get our word
dynamite from this Greek word *dunamis*).

We preach Christ—He's "dynamite" indeed!
We preach Christ—the "knowledge" that we need!
  We preach Christ—God, send a heav'nly shower
  Of *knowledge* and *power* for this *crisis hour!*

God pleads with workers and laymen to rise;
The time has come to evangelize!
  This world in darkness of sin needs light,
  To do this right, we need "dynamite!"

The dynamite of *truth*—God's light divine,
The dynamite of *love*—O let it shine!
The dynamite of *power*—a heav'nly shower
Of *knowledge* and *power* for this *crisis hour!*

Life's Great Positives

"Eliminate the negative, accentuate the positive."

"Unless you cultivate a cheerful, happy, grateful frame of mind, Satan will eventually lead you captive at his will."—*Testimonies,* vol. 1, p. 704.

"Nothing tends more to promote health of body and of soul than does a spirit of gratitude and praise. It is a positive duty to resist melancholy, discontented thoughts and feelings—as much a duty as it is to pray."—*The Ministry of Healing,* p. 251.

Are you sometimes shocked to find you have a "negative
      mind"?
A Christian always should be known as the "positive" kind!
Because, in real Christianity, in God's divine design,
The cross is not a "minus," but instead *a true "plus" sign!*
It adds to life true values and it adds the sweetest peace,
Adds vict'ry over vices and from sin it brings release.

      The Ten Commandments are much more than merely
            "Thou shalt *not"!*
      They're really precious promises so many folk forgot.
      While sinners boldly murder or they steal, for sin they
            will,
      The Lord repeats His promises: "My child *'Thou* shalt
            not kill';
      I'll give you love instead of hate and keep you free from
            sin;
      In all your lifetime struggles I will give you power to
            win."

It's not enough to work our gardens, pulling out the weeds,
For we must cultivate the soil and plant pure precious seeds.
Where weeds once grew, rare roses bloom so fair, so sweet
and red;
Where sin once ruled the heart, the King of kings now
reigns instead.
We "don't do this," we "can't do that," and do you ask me
why?
Because we're busy "fitting up" for mansions in the sky!

But while we're getting ready for our home beyond the
skies,
We live our very best on earth and win life's purest
prize.
Christ added up the Ten Commandments—what, pray,
did He find?
This: "Thou shalt love the Lord thy God with all thy heart
and mind,
And love thy neighbor as thyself—on these two hang
all ten!"
Ah! These are life's great positives—*love to God* and
love to men!

Assignment

We need participation
As we serve the human race.
And God in my creation
Has prepared a special place.

That the World May Know

We've come to this great world session,
  With humble and heartfelt confession.
    The church has been given possession
      Of truth that the world must know!

We've come for worship and humble prayer.
  We've come with knowledge that we must share—
    Are we concerned? How much do we care?
      Surely our actions will show!

We've come for revival of faith and zeal;
  Our lusterless love we cannot conceal.
    We've come to seek power the *truth* to reveal!
      This is the work to be done!

What is the truth that the world must know,
  Through literature and the radio,
    And witness of Christians with hearts aglow?
      Is it some*thing?* or some*one?*

Not merely the truth of historical facts
  Or messages found in our literature racks
    But a modern version of the book of Acts.

"I am the *way*" Christ said one day;
  "I am the *truth*" that you must convey;
    "I am the *life*" you must live alway!

      This is the task that must be done
      By the church on earth ere the set of sun!

SECTION 4

Prayer and Thanksgiving

"Rivers"

" "The man who believes in me, as the scripture said, will have rivers of living water flowing from his inmost heart.' " John 7:38, Phillips.*

> Make us, dear Lord, real rivers of life,
> Flowing forth in a world of strife.
> Mankind is dying in sin's sad state;
> Help us to heal the wounds of hate.
>
> Make us, O Lord, rich rivers of peace,
> To bring to men a sweet release

From civil wars that rage within,
And vict'ry over ev'ry sin.

Make us, O Lord, great rivers of power,
To face the challenge of each hour,
To meet the needs of this tragic time,
And do Thy glorious work sublime!

Make us, dear Lord, sweet rivers of love,
With rivers of kindness fresh from above;
To heal the hurts of hearts at strife
And show a better way of life.

Rivers, dear Lord, not dried up brooks;
Rivers, of smiles, kind words, and looks.
Rivers, not merely trickling streams,
Rivers to match our fondest dreams!

Rivers of wisdom for aged and youth;
Rivers of pages of printed truth.
Rivers of influence, like rare perfume,
Cheering men's hearts in a world of gloom!

Rivers to flood the world with light;
Rivers of helpfulness day and night.
Keep our hearts' rivers pure and sweet,
With no choked channels of deceit!

Rivers of blessings to young and old,
Till we walk at last on those streets of gold.
Rivers of peace in this world of strife,
Till we drink at last from Thy river of life!

The Brotherhood of Burning Hearts

"Did not our hearts burn within us as He talked with us?"
Luke 24:32.

Teach us, dear Lord, what we should learn.
Come as the flaming fire to burn;
    Come as the wind to stir and cleanse
    And save us from man's current trends.
    On Thee our destiny depends.
Come as the light, Thy truth reveal;
Come, Holy Spirit, with Thy zeal.
    Come with convicting power divine,
    Till we are truly, wholly Thine.
    And then, like John, we'll burn and shine
And serve Thee, Lord, with one desire,
With flaming tongues of living fire,
    And sharing what Thy love imparts
    With new techniques and heav'nly arts—
    A brotherhood of burning hearts!

God's Call Divine

I thank Thee, God, for Thy call divine
To live and serve as a child of Thine.
Give us, we pray Thee, the mind of Christ,
To faithfully meet our daily tryst;
Hearts that will rev'rently worship Thee,
And minds to fathom life's mystery;
Bodies to serve Thee with love and power,
And wills to obey Thee hour by hour.
This is the service we want to give—
This is the life that we long to live.

The Crowning Evidence

Columbus discovered a great new world
And o'er it the Spanish flag unfurl'd,
But when he got home the stories he told—
His fabulous tales of people and gold—
All seemed fantastic, so wild and so weird,
They would not believe, but instead only jeered.

Columbus was desperate—oh, what could he do
To prove that his wonderful stories were true?
And then as he pondered he thought a great thought—
The six North American Indians he'd brought;
He called them forth from the hold of the ship,
And here was the proof of his marvelous trip!

Their heads wore strange feathers, their bodies war paint,
The people were frightened, some ready to faint.
But now as they gazed on that fantastic sight
They knew he'd discovered a new world, all right.
Those skeptical people, plagued by doubts, fear, and strife,
Saw his *crowning proof in a new kind of life!*

Now our jeering age of sneering, doubting peoples
Must *see transformed lives*—not just our church steeples!

Unfinished Business

(After an Autumn Council.)

Dear God, in all earth's mission lands
    Thy world work still is incomplete.
Empower our weak, though willing, hands,
    Put wings, we pray, upon our feet.

Within our homes, our minds, our hearts,
　　A noble work Thou hast begun.
We'll see, through power Thy grace imparts,
　　A finished work by set of sun.

Thy work for man goes on apace—
　　Unfinished business everywhere,
Redeeming this decadent race.
　　Complete the task—this is our prayer!

The Challenge of Our Day

"Without adventure civilization is in full decay"—so is Christianity!

"My father fought for you, and adventured his life far, and delivered you out of the hand of Midian." Judges 9:17.

While meeting here to plan and pray,
　　We turn to God, to humbly ask
To see the challenge of our day,
　　And face our great unfinished task.

Not just to see a vision new,
　　But we must implement God's plan;
To venture far in all we do,
　　And reach each home and ev'ry man!

The sunset burns across the sky
　　Declaring this is time's last hour.
To save earth's lost before they die,
　　We plead for Pentecostal power.

Anoint our eyes, inspire our souls
To plan our work and reach our goals.

Two of Paul's Prayers
(Ephesians 1:15-23; Ephesians 3:14-21.)

At first Paul prayed that he might *see*,
And then he prayed that he might *be*.
He asked at first for *revelation*,
And then he sought for *realization*.
He asked for Heaven's *light* to shine,
And then he longed for *life* divine.
He prayed for God's *enlightenment*,
Then longed for God's *enablement*
To *know* ourselves that we may grow
And then *to be* just what we know.
He asked God's power to work *for* us,
Then for that power to work *in* us,
You in Christ and Christ in you
Be seen and felt in all we do.
He asked *to know God's holy power*,
And then *experience* it each hour.

Yes, Paul prayed first that he might see,
And then he prayed that he might be.

Thankfulness

Nothing compares to the spirit of praise
To help keep us healthy all of our days.
Not only our bodies but mind and soul
Are richer by far when the heart has control.
A "merry heart" truly has healing power
To bless and sweeten each passing hour.
May all of us practice this healing art
That does so much to the human heart.

"Watch Unto Prayer"

Our modern youth seem unaware
Of dangers lurking everywhere.
Torn bodies, twisted steel and minds—
What is it each autopsy finds?

The devil plays the game of life
With young and old, husband and wife.
Behold the daily, tragic toll
Of everyone who sells his soul!

Each day, each one must make a choice.
Oh, let us heed God's warning voice.
Do not neglect, with flippant air,
The call of Christ: "Watch unto prayer."

On Giving Thanks

Dear God, before we eat this lovely meal,
We humbly pause to tell Thee how we feel.
We thank Thee for these precious friends, so kind,
Whose opened doors of home and heart and mind
Invite us share their hospitality
Within the circle of their family.

We thank Thee for the many colors fair
Which Thou didst place in all foods rich and rare,
To please our eyes as we sit down to eat.
We thank Thee, too, for all the flavors sweet,
Which please and satisfy our palate's taste,
When we relax and do not eat in haste.

We thank Thee for the energy we find
In all our food, to nourish heart and mind
And keep our bodies healthy and so strong
That we can sing with joy the victor's song.
We thank Thee for real culinary art,
Which helps one eat with glad and happy heart.

We thank Thee, Father, for this food so good,
And for this sweet and blessed brotherhood.
We ask Thee now to draw so very near
That we can feel Thy hallowed presence here.
O bless this home where we, as guests, reside,
May peace and Thy sweet Spirit here abide.

Moral Icebergs

"There are moral icebergs in our churches. There are plenty of
formalists who can make an imposing display, but cannot shine
as lights in the world."—*Christian Service*, p. 40.

O Lord, how selfish and how cold our hearts,
　　How small each prayer,
　　When we compare
　　　　Ourselves with Thee.
　　　　O may we *see*
And *feel* the flames of fire Thy love imparts!

How weak our efforts, Lord, how low our goals,
　　Compared with Thine.
　　May fire divine
　　　　Burn out all vice,
　　　　Melt all the ice,
Releasing frozen assets of our souls!

SECTION 5

Nature's Mirror

"*So wide was Christ's view of truth, so extended His teaching, that every phase of nature was employed in illustrating truth.*"—Christ's Object Lessons, *p. 20.*

Springtime Miracles

So many springtime miracles we see
In lily ponds or flowering bush and tree.
We find in leaf and bud, on spring parade,
The resurrected power of God displayed.

We're thrilled to see such beauty, pure and bright,
Rise from these filthy waters, clean and white.
Will our lives be as lovely and be found
As uncontaminated from the world around?

Treasures at Sunrise

The Lord awakened me this dawn
To see fresh emeralds on the lawn.
A glorious sunrise blessed my eyes
With one more sweet divine surprise;
A flock of golden-tinted sheep
Repaid me for my loss of sleep.
But soon those clouds had turned to gray,
With swiftly moving dawn of day.

God taught this lesson once again:
That treasures which He gives to men
Are often seen at break of day,
But soon are gone if we delay.
I would have lost through "slothful sleep"
My flock of golden-tinted sheep,
And missed the emeralds on the lawn
By heeding not the drums of dawn.

Man's poverty of soul, it seems
Will only come to him who dreams!

Some Secrets for a Successful
Sabbath School Garden

Some secrets I will gladly share
On planting gardens sweet and fair.
Within your church, your Sabbath school,
'Twill help you keep the golden rule;
And if you work with all your heart
And use techniques with heavenly art,
Your school a model school will be,
A model for all men to see.

The thing to do—now, listen please—
First, plant five rows of these sweet *peas:*
    P for *p*romptness, *p*atience, *p*ersecution, too,
    Then *p*eace and *p*iety will bloom for you.

These *peas* will be much beautified,
With seeds of *squash* right by their side:
    Squash gossip, *squash* indifference—and how!
    Squash tardiness, *squash* suspicion now!
    Squash childishness—grow up and be a man,
    Your garden should be useful in God's plan.

Five rows of *turnips* look so good
And surely bless the brotherhood.
    Turn up for meetings, *turn up* with a smile.
    Turn up with ideas new and worth while.
    Turn up with helping hands, willing to work,
    Turn up with determination and never shirk.

Five rows of *lettuce* will help too,
To do the things we ought to do.

Let *us* be loyal and meet obligations.
Let *us* be true to our task for the nations.
Let *us* respect one another and seek
To be always faithful and be always meek.

A Sabbath school garden like this, you'll agree,
Makes much better gardens for the world to see.

The Stars Still Shine

It's such a thrill to rise at night
    And see the stars still shine.
One glimpse of that transcendent sight
    Revives this heart of mine.

I watch the constellations speed
    Along their ordered course.
It seems the universal need
    Is met by universal force.

Whence cometh all this mighty power
    To guide Arcturus with his sons,
Unceasingly, hour after hour,
    Each on the course he runs?

I contemplate this vast array
    Of wisdom, power, and love;
I'm stirred to see this grand display
    That spans the heavens above.

My finite mind is filled with awe
    Before such glory spread abroad;
I find a universal law
    That all things are upheld by God.

SECTION 6

Life's Priorities

Life's Priorities

"The things that matter most must not be at the mercy of the things that matter least."

> The things that matter most in life
>   Provide the heart's perennial feast;
> Unless they're placed, mid earth's mad strife,
>   Beneath the things that matter least!

Does Every Man Have His Price?

"The greatest want of the world is the want of men—men who
will not be bought or sold, men who in their inmost souls are true
and honest, men who do not fear to call sin by its right name, men
whose conscience is as true to duty as the needle to the pole, men
who will stand for the right though the heavens fall."—*Education,*
p. 57.

<blockquote>
While I was still a little lad,
One day I overheard my dad
  Hold forth about the human race.
  He thought it was a great disgrace
    The way folks stooped to any vice,
    And sold their virtue for a price.

For fifty years my dad's been dead—
I still recall those words he said,
  That "ev'ry person has a price."
  I did not think it true or nice!
    Since then I've studied human kind
    And I will tell you what I find.

Sin is so subtle, yet has such power,
That few folks know the day or hour
  When they sell out—they have their price—
  Perhaps, at first, a little vice.
    Perhaps a little "social sin"
    That snapped their self-control within.

Some sell out for "a social drink,"
Some sell out quicker than they think.
  A cigarette—the price of some,
  A thrill, Pied Piper's flute and drum,
</blockquote>

The pretty lights, a cap and bell.
They sell their souls to pay for—hell!

It seems that Satan has some plan
To try and lure and tempt each man,
  Then ere he knows it, man is caught,
  Entwined as in a web, his lot.
    Some buy strange fashions of the day,
    And what a price they have to pay!

To be like all the world around,
This is the subtlest lure I've found.
  The god of fashion rules mankind
  And through mass media molds man's mind.
    To ape the world—is this your goal?
    The quickest way to starve your soul!

It cannot be our Father's plan,
To bare our nakedness to man,
  And thus become the devil's lure,
  To make the thoughts of men impure.
    I blush to see the trend—how crude
    To show off nude, lewd pulchritude.

The Christian women of our land
Should show the world just where they stand.
  They stand for modesty in dress;
  And character, we must confess,
    Is oft revealed by what we wear,
    So we must choose our clothes with care.

There is one thing we can't forget—
The last temptation Israel met

Before they reached the Promised Land
Was sexual vice—the Moab brand.
　Again God's remnant church must face
　This crowning sin of all our race!

I've found my dear old dad was right,
Each human has his price all right.
　The only safety then, I'm sure,
　The only way we can endure—
　　Receive the power God will impart
　　When Jesus reigns within your heart!

Our only hope, then, if we're wise,
With sin we will not compromise.
　For when we can't be "bought or sold,"
　Our value far surpasses gold.
　　Henceforth our virtue can't be priced—
　　We serve and worship only Christ!

O may we hear the prophet's voice
To guide us in each crucial choice!

Heaven, a Worthy Goal

Since Father's kingdom is our greatest goal,
This high objective radiates the soul.
　We make this worried world a better place
　When faith and love keep shining through each face.
For with a smile no one is ever bored,
And faith in God in many is restored.
　Pursue thy goal with ev'ry fleeting breath—
　An aimless life is but a living death!

Man's Real Failure

There's only one failure in any life,
  In spite of opinions of friends or foes.
The one real failure in all of man's strife
  Is *not* to be *true to the best one knows!*

Terminology Is Not Enough

It's not terminology
  That saves us from sin;
It's Jesus our Lord
  When He lives within.
It's the great love of God,
  With its matchless art,
That wins other men
  As it flows through our heart.

Why She Wept

The off'ring had been taken;
  One little girl near by
Was obviously quite shaken,
  So we asked, "What makes her cry?"

Her little playmate then replied,
  And made us *think* then *sing;*
She said, "The reason why she cried—
  She had no offering."

'Twas then my own eyes filled with tears,
  Shamed by my grasping greed.
When selfishness all disappears,
  With love we'll meet each need!

Faith

"Believe on the Lord Jesus Christ, and thou shalt be saved."
Acts 16:31.

Have faith in *someone*,
Not just in *something*.
Faith in your King
And what He has done!

"Love Divine, All Loves Excelling"

All maternal love praised by the sages;
All fraternal love on hist'ry's pages,
All paternal love of all the ages,
Are all as a tiny, trickling rill,
Compared to the love of the Father's will,
In giving His Son to die for earth's ill.

We may eulogize love with our choicest rhyme,
We might study this love through all of time,
But never can fathom God's love sublime!
He gave us His Son to die on a tree,
He gave us a Saviour to set man free;
That love was so great it included me.

Despite earth's rebellion, God's love remains,
His love will finally remove sin's stains,
This infinite love eternally reigns!

The Power of Hope

Man has no other power with which to cope
With fear and doubt but *faith* and *love* and *hope!*

My Best for God

"I will place no value on anything I have or may possess except in relation to the kingdom of Christ. If anything I have will advance the interests of that kingdom, it shall be given away or kept, only as by giving or keeping it I may promote the glory of Him to whom I owe all my hopes in time and eternity."—DR. DAVID LIVINGSTONE.

> Are we doing our best?
>   Are we giving our all?
> Are we standing life's test?
>   Are we heeding God's call?
>
> Are we seeing a wraith?
>   Are we spreading our fear?
> Are we sharing our faith?
>   Are we giving out cheer?
>
> Are we singing a song
>   While we're walking abroad?
> Are we fighting all wrong?
>   Are we living for God?

Writing Positively

"[Christ spake] as one having authority, and not as the scribes." Matt. 7:29.

> Until you've had a real toothache,
>   And felt its pangs of pain,
> Then it would be a big mistake
>   For you to use your brain
> And try to write a book about
> This thing of which you have some doubt.

And yet some authors take their pen
   And write that "God is dead."
It does not help their fellow men
   To hear the doubts they spread.
What prompts such people to dethrone
A God they have not really known?

The man who has a toothache reels
   With pain—you understand?
And when a man knows God he feels
   A power that is *firsthand!*
When you write books, then write about
The things of which you have no doubt.

But no one cares to have you show
   The many things *you do not know,*
But when you've felt God's lifting power
You have a message for this hour!

Hope Is My Window

Eternity a treasure house divine,
And hope the window I may claim as mine,
Through which my eager eyes may dimly see
The precious things God has prepared for me.

One Thing Needful

With eloquence of angels I might talk,
   The wisdom of the ages might impart;
Though to a martyr's death I choose to walk,
   'Tis worthless without love within my heart!

Accent on Health

Health Is Harmony

If "health is harmony," as we are told,
　　Then make good health your daily goal;
And let no civil war unfold
　　Within your body, mind, or soul.

Inside your mouth put nothing bad,
　　To make your mind or "tummy" ache;
And never worry or get mad,
　　Wrong words and thoughts you must forsake.

With body, mind, and soul at peace,
  You now can learn life's highest art.
With harmony, health will increase
  The pleasures of your happy heart!

Exercise

Is exercise required by girls
  As much as by our boys?
Of course, and not spasmodic whirls,
  But *faithfulness,* not noise.

Consistency's a jewel here
  As in all things we do.
The way some exercise, I fear,
  Will not make them "like new."

By exercising *ev'ry day*
  Your muscles will grow strong.
Don't get *suntan* the "one-day way"—
  That's *sunburn* and that's wrong!

Guard Your Health—Shun All Vices

The *health* of ev'ry girl and boy
Improves life's work, increases joy!

That's why we want each boy and girl
To guard health like a precious pearl.

A drop of poison never take
In any form, for your health's sake.

Oh, poisoned alcohol we dread—
It kills all life, preserves the dead.

The devil in solution, see—
Distilled damnation, misery!

It does not mix with gasoline,
Behold the drunkard's wrecked machine.

It does not mix with music's tongue,
Our Stephen Foster died so young.

It does not mix with human brains,
What tragedies it brings—what pains!

That's why I vowed, when just a boy,
I'd fight each vice that steals life's joy.

To ev'ry youth I'd say right now—
It's time for you to make that vow!

Seven Friendly Doctors

Seven friendly "doctors" wait
    Each day to heed our beck and call.
And if you ask me how they rate,
    I think they're greatest of them all.

Sunshine, Sleep, Pure Food, and Air,
    Oh! What a combination!
Water, Exercise, and Prayer—
    Why, these could save the nation!

Prescription for Health

A simple diet with a merry mind,
Two helpful hands, a tongue that's always kind;
Deep breathing of pure air (still free from tax);
While eating meals, and after work, relax!

Two smiling eyes to prove you still can laugh;
Live simpler lives and cut your bills in half.
A task you love, a conscience crystal clear;
A heart at rest, a mind that's free from fear.

Use water freely, more within, without;
Have faith in God and give no place to doubt.
Then exercise your body, mind, and soul;
Look up and keep your eyes upon life's goal!

Good Nutrition With Better Breakfasts

If you'll make your breakfasts better
    And not eat between your meals,
You can be a real *go-getter*—
    It's amazing how one feels!

Take this tip—eat foods with color,
    Look for yellows, reds, and green.
When you *don't,* life is much duller,
    When you *do,* life is serene.

Eat more fruits with colors tempting,
    Eat more nuts—they'll keep you strong.
Good nutrition is attempting
    To help *you* live *well* and *long!*

Ulcers

Most of your ulcers develop, I hear,
Less from your food than from things that you fear:
Not from the victuals you happen to chew,
As much as from things that are eating on you!

Physical Checkup

Our motor cars we often check
Because we would prevent a wreck.
We're very careful how we drive,
We want to "bring 'em back alive."
We drive until we hear some noise,
Then call on service station boys,
"Look, fill 'er up and check the oil;
And check the battery and the coil.
And better check the water, too,
And check the tires, though they're brand new.
If you see anything that's bad
Just fix it and we'll all be glad."

'Tis thus, you see, we check our car,
Because we want it to go far.
We think about our cars, indeed,
But look—*what does your body need?*
Let's check our human body, too;
Just think of what it has to do!
It needs some tender loving care,
If you want it to give long wear.
So check your body's daily need,
And then in life you should succeed!
And then, on annual checkup day,
The "piper" you'll not have "to pay!"

God's Food Plan for Man

When God made man
He had a plan
To keep him happy, well, and strong.
And if man would
Eat what he should
He'd never hear "the death knell gong."

God made man's home
'Neath heaven's dome,
With nuts, fruits, herbs, and grains to eat.
The colors fair,
And flavors rare
Made ev'ry meal a royal treat!

Temptations came,
Oh! What a shame,
Man disobeyed his loving God;
Driv'n from his home,
He still must roam
Upon earth's dusty sin-cursed sod.

A great new plan
God has for man,
With paradise he lost, restored;
We'll eat the good
The way we should,
And God will ever be adored!

Self-control
or
Digging Graves With Teeth

Some people dig their graves with their own teeth,
And then their friends must buy another wreath.
What price is paid for ev'ry pound of fat,
(Enough I'm sure for many a brand-new hat).
To kill yourself you do not need a gun,
Just laugh at self-control and eat for fun!

But when the faithful doctor comes along
It's not a laughing joke, but one sad song.
He shakes his head as nature takes her toll,
And says, "He died for lack of self-control."
Learn this while young—regardless how one feels,
Don't gorge yourself or eat between your meals!

Stay well and strong so you can reach life's goal;
This you can do if you use self-control!

Gossip vs. Personal Knowledge

What right can any person claim
    To talk against a good man's goal,
Defame his character and name,
    Yet never knew the great man's soul?

When those of us who know that man,
    With such a personal knowledge, too,
And those of us who know his plan
    Rebel at gossip that's not true.

The doubter likewise has no right
   To spread his awful spate of hate,
And talk against the God of light,
   Who leads us through the gate called "strait."

Why war with God in mortal strife—
The God who gives a better life?
He may not wish with God to dwell,
But why lead other folks to hell?
A man is mad, he's vicious, wild,
To shake the faith of even a child.
Better to hang upon a pole
Than be the cause of one lost soul.

   What motive prompts a doubter so,
   To write of things he does not know?

Wrinkles

A prune is full of wrinkles sad,
   Though it be young or old,
But some folks get their wrinkles bad
   When they should not, I'm told.

The wrinkles form upon your face
   With anger, grief, or frown.
A prune gets wrinkles every place—
   Don't be a "prune" or clown.

Keep sweet and smile, then on your brow
   The peace of God will rest.
The "crow's feet" wrinkles some form now,
   Prove smiles, not frowns, are best.

SECTION 8

Worthy of Tribute

To H. M. S. Richards

The "Voice" of the Voice of Prophecy

The pioneers are not all dead—
I point to one who forged ahead,
 Who blazed a trail
 And did not fail!
 Since we were neighbors many years,
  I know the man,
  I know his plan,
 I've heard his prayers, I've seen his tears!
A man who sought the cosmic wires
To flash the Infinite's desires.

We honor him who dreamed the dream
Of making Christ his life's great theme.
  And men rejoice
  To hear his voice
 Re-echo from a thousand hills.
  He met his tryst—
  He lifts up Christ,
 And gives the world a million thrills,
Around the trails of earth he's trod,
And says to all, "Have faith in God."

So we commemorate the morn
The Voice of Prophecy was born.
  Lives there a man
  With finer plan
 To help truth's banner be unfurled?
  For ev'ry week
  The voice did speak
 Its ringing message for the world,

And ev'ry broadcast still imparts
Rich blessings to all hungry hearts!

He used the power of printer's ink
To help to make the millions think,
 For in his dream
 He saw a scheme—
A Bible correspondence school
 So aged or youth
 Could learn the truth
By mail—another useful tool.
The wondrous plan has proved its worth—
The largest radio school on earth!

For many wondrous, fruitful years
His flaming faith has conquered fears,
 And men have heard
 The living Word
At home or trav'ling far abroad.
 From silvered throat
 The matchless note
Of truth and hope and love of God,
Has sounded forth to urge all men
Prepare, for Christ will come again.

The Touchstone of Honor

"Many a man . . . possesses powers which, if called into action, would raise him to an equality with the world's most honored men. . . . When the disciples came forth from the Saviour's training, they were no longer ignorant and uncultured. They had become like Him in mind and character."—*The Desire of Ages,* p. 250.

God's Warrior Rests

(A tribute to Elder H. T. Elliott.)

"I have fought a good fight, I have finished my course, I have kept the faith: henceforth there is laid up for me a crown of righteousness, which the Lord, the righteous judge, shall give me at that day: and not to me only, but unto all them also that love his appearing." 2 Tim. 4:7, 8.

Another stalwart has fallen,
　　Another leader now sleeps.
His journey of life is over,
　　His record an angel now keeps.

He rests from his heavy labors,
　　The deeds of his life live on
In the lives of ten thousand others,
　　In mem'ries of him now gone.

We're proud of his noble achievements,
　　The wonderful things he has done
For the youth of this mighty movement,
　　For the battles and vic'tries won.

The torch of truth he has carried,
　　We've taken from his tired hands;
We'll help to fulfill his vision
　　Of enlightening the mission lands.

We've come to pay our tribute
　　Of love, respect, and esteem.
We see in his lifetime of service
　　The measure of love supreme.

What rich rewards await him,
  With his fighting gear all laid down,
When the Master comes in His glory
  And exchanges the cross for the crown!

To Elder and Mrs. Frank D. Wells

on Their Sixty-fifth Wedding Anniversary
September 2, 1967

(P.S. to the poem on your Golden Wedding Day,
September 2, 1952.)

I thought my song was ended nearly fifteen years ago,
But now I sing a stanza of your Golden Afterglow.
The years have slipped by quickly, and you've found so
  much to do,
With Sabbath school Investment and the funds Ingathered,
  too;
You've been an inspiration to your loved ones and your
  friends,
You've helped so many others seek that life that never ends.
So after sixty-five grand years of pure, sweet wedded life,
We're glad that we can once again pronounce you man
  and wife.
As future years unfold, we know the best is yet to come—
You'll walk those golden streets throughout the blest
  millennium.
Your health restored, your youth renewed—your joys will
  never cease.
What rich rewards await you in that land of love and peace!

A Tribute to My Wife

(February 5, 1920, Friends; February 5, 1921, Engaged;
February 5, 1923, Married.)

A tribute I would pay my wife
    Upon our day of days;
She's brought such joy into my life
    That I must sing her praise.

Our friendship's ties for fifty years
    Have brought their rich increase;
Her words, like music to my ears,
    Have filled my heart with peace.

She's helped make home a little bit
    Of heaven here on earth;
Her ready wit, I will admit,
    Added life's needed mirth.

Her artistry, her cooking too,
    Her music charmed my soul;
And honesty—she was true blue;
    She reached for God's great goal.

Her patient love subdued the beast
    That lurked within my life;
Her sweetness, a perennial feast,
    Makes me adore my wife!

And so this tribute, I would pay
Upon this anniversary day!

My Valentine

They told me all the nicest things
    And words that were divine
Had long ago been spoken
    About my valentine.

But I began to scratch my head
    And I massaged my heart
To see if I could not squeeze out
    One nice new sharpened dart.

And so I whispered sweet and low
    With Flo's eyes meeting mine,
"If I take you around the world,
    Will you be my valentine?"

The look she gave me was benign,
    Her words life's sweetest wine.
She said, "Adlai, I now resign—
    You are my valentine."

The Lay Activities Leader

Sparkling and twinkling
    And tinkling with cheer,
Bubbling with laughter,
    Not trembling with fear;
Sharing his courage,
    With tasks he must cope,
Inspiring the laymen
    With faith, zeal, and hope!

To President and Mrs. Richard Nixon

on the first anniversary of his presidency,
January 20, 1969-January 20, 1970.

Why should we wait 'till men are dead,
    Before we bring our wreath of flowers—
Then quote the famous words they've said
    And eulogize their gifted powers?

Who was it said the kindly word,
    When Dick was reeling from life's blows?
Was it Pat's lovely voice he heard?
    Was it her poetry or prose?

How many men, crushed by defeat,
    Have been inspired to try again;
Their tempered steel improved by heat—
    Life's fiercest fires forge finest men!

What battles Washington had lost,
    When Valley Forge left one more scar;
Yet he fought on at frightful cost—
    He lost the battles, won the war!

Remember Lincoln's sorry plight
    When Stanton cried, "The fool! How long?"
But Lincoln said, "He must be right;
    I've never known him to be wrong."

So now when modern tongues are tart
    And hurl each caustic epithet,
Like Lincoln, Nixon has the art
    To say kind words he won't regret!

The world is being taught again
    This vital and forgotten fact:
Time's noblest and time's greatest men,
    Know how to speak and how to act!

The essence and quintessence, too,
    Of wisdom we could call sublime,
Is know *the right thing* we should do,
    Done *the right way* at *the right time!*

Will Nixon prize his priceless power
    And ride the waves of stress and strife?
He is, God grant, man of the hour,
    Wrought in time's crucible of life!

Nixon's genius for the wholesome,
    His passion for the good and right,
With faith in what we could become—
    He guides US through our moral night!

    My tribute now I humbly bring,
    And Richard Nixon's praises sing:
    He's captain of our ship of State—
    God bless him and his charming mate!

Living and Dying for Others

(Written at the request of R. C. Thomas and dedicated
to Joe Hunt.)

On a friendly, fruitful Iowa farm,
With all of its joys, its peace, and charm,
The Hunt fam'ly lived, without alarm.
They did their work and they feared no harm.

But, one beautiful, sunny, summer day,
The father and son were out making hay,
When the father was killed that tragic day,
In a very sacrificial way!

Joe had been driving, though he was young,
And somehow fell on the wagon tongue.
The horses were frightened and ran unstrung,
While Joe's boyish hands to the wagon clung.

The father noticed his son's sad plight,
And raced to the scene with all his might.
He grabbed at a horse, but in the mad flight
He was crushed by the wagon and died that night.

That year Joe, who was only ten,
Said that his dad was the "best of men."
He decided to live for God, and then,
He'd live with his precious dad again!

Now Joe has grown up, no longer a lad,
But still wants to "live and die like his dad."
He works with his soul and is never sad,
For he's living each day to make others glad!

Joe loves his church, he's loyal and true
And proud of the work he's called to do.
He wants to see the great task through,
And see his dad in the earth made new!

To the Honorable Jerry Pettis, M.C.

A man of action—may his tribe increase;
A man of honor and a man of peace.
As true to duty as needle to pole,
A man who has no price tag on his soul!

His name's on the plaque that was left on the moon;
His committee's achievements, our country's boon.
An earnest public servant, sharp and keen,
A man that's in the vanguard of the national scene!

He reads a book a day, in step with time.
I can't state his accomplishments in rhyme.
Since I pay taxes in the Golden State,
I'm proud to have him represent my fate.

A man of deep conviction you can trust,
A man with sympathy but fair and just.
A man who wins his races, full of pep,
He's going places with a steady step!

To Jerry Pettis my tribute I pay,
And many happy returns of the day!

Congratulations to All Ingathering Partners

The Gen'ral Conf'rence brethren in our weekly convocations
Heard good reports, so voted to send congratulations
To leaders—union, conf'rence, church, and institutions,
    too—
For great Ingath'ring progress in the work we're called
    to do.

We're partners in this mighty task, we're workers, too,
    with God;
We're partners as we "lengthen cords" in many lands
    abroad.
We're partners as we "strengthen stakes" at home, a work
    of worth—
This mighty laymen's movement is the greatest work on
    earth!

We want to see the message swell into the great loud cry.
We want to see the end of war and sin, from which men
    die.
We want to see the Master come and from pain bring
    release;
We want to see our precious Lord, the glorious Prince of
    Peace!

And when He comes, what will it mean to see him face
    to face
And hear Him say, "Well done," and feel the power of
    love and grace?
Ah, then we'll see the harvest! O how many precious souls
Will stand upon the sea of glass, because we reached our
    goals!

Then arm in arm with Jesus, we'll walk those streets of
     gold,
Our minds electrified to know we'll ne'er again grow old.
And what a matchless thrill 'twill be, whene'er we chance
     to meet
Someone who'll say, "I'm here in heav'n because you worked
     my street!

"You told me of a better world with joys forevermore;
"You never knew the hope you brought when you knocked
     on my door!
"And now I'll live forever in this glorious earth made new.
"I join the Gen'ral Conf'rence in thanking God and you!"

A Tribute to Doctors Malin
and
The Medical Group Foundation

A tribute I bring,
The praises I sing
Of a grand group of medical men.
By faith they began
To serve needy man—
Their story deserves a far better pen.

First a clinic small—
Faith and skill, that's all—
Some thought the work was doomed to fail;
But love and boundless zeal,
Made their strange appeal
And turned defeat into a marvelous tale.

Today in hospitals three,
Five hundred work with glee—
The budget two million dollars a year.
A wonderful team
Fulfilling a dream
Of service sharing their faith, hope, and cheer.

Our tribute we bring,
Our praises we sing
Of Doctors Malin, their helpers, and friends;
The blessings they've brought,
The miracles wrought,
Will be told in that day when all sickness ends!

A Tribute to Our Firemen

(Dedicated to Lt. Charles Ferdock, of the Hillandale Fire Depart-
ment, my roommate in the Washington Sanitarium and Hospital,
January 26 to 30, 1970.)

I'd like to pay a tribute to the firemen of our land;
They are dedicated workers, they're a brave courageous
band.
They daily risk their lives and labor on without surcease,
Protecting the community—they're guardians of our peace!

They face the flaming fires and smoke while saving young
and old,
The story of their noble deeds has not been fully told.
God bless these faithful firemen and their wives and children, too,
I pay my tribute to these men—they're noble, brave, and
true!

The Christian Home

As long as there are homes where virtue reigns,
And peace and joy shine through the windowpanes;
Where faith and love and discipline combine
To make a little world of trust divine;
Where houses change to homes and joys abide,
And loyalty and love are locked inside;
Where every member of the family vies
To show how much he cares through smiling eyes;
Where faithful, helping hands and willing feet
Unite to make their happiness complete—
With homes where kindness walks across the sills,
The country can recover from its gravest ills.
Where homes are harbors of our heart's desires,
And daily prayers rekindle altar fires—
Though nations war and men in darkness grope,
While there are homes like these there still is hope!

A Christian Witness

A Christian witness is a man
    Who shares what he has learned
About the glorious gospel plan,
    For which his own heart yearned.

A witness is a "martyr," true,
    This was the word in Greek;
He is a real imparter, too,
    Of love that all men seek.

A witness tells just what he knows,
    And states the thrills he feels!

He can't describe an unknown rose,
   Or fragrance it conceals.

But should the Rose of Sharon bloom
   In beauty in his heart,
His witness then can pierce earth's gloom
   With heav'nly charm and art.

A witness cannot give away
   What he does not possess.
When he knows Christ he can convey
   Real hope and happiness.

A witness shows his true concern
   With unfeigned friendliness,
His love must yearn for souls and burn
   All trace of selfishness.

A witness must be careful not
   To witness to himself;
Some folks failed here, for they forgot
   And placed Christ on a shelf.

Is Christ the center of our theme?
   The Pearl so highly priced?
Fulfillment of our fondest dream—
   Our Witness—Jesus Christ!

We witness to a Person, then,
   Not doctrines, facts, or creed;
We introduce our Friend to men.
   He meets all human needs!

SECTION 9

Memorable Occasions

Memorable Occasions

Each Thanksgiving, Christmas, and New Year's Day
  Is a happy occasion and, we confess,
Provides us a cheerful chance to convey
  Our wish for your health and your happiness!

THANKSGIVING

Ah! "Nothing tends more" to improve your health *
    Than a grateful and cheerful frame of mind;
A simple, trusting faith is greater wealth
    Than all other treasures you'll ever find!
(So let's make *every day* a day of *thankfulness!*)

MERRY CHRISTMAS

A merry Christmas is a gladsome time,
    For young and old join the angels and sing
Of infinite myst'ries—the Babe sublime—
    The hope and good news of the new-born King!
(His birth in our hearts makes a merry Christmas daily!)

HAPPY NEW YEAR

With thankfulness thrilling our minds and hearts,
    With hope and true peace "to men of good will";
We're eager to see what the new year imparts.
    We pray your life with love God will infill!
(This will make a happy new year for you!)

SEASON'S GREETINGS

We're glad to bring these Greetings to our friends,
    And our best wishes for the coming days.
We hope you find God's peace that never ends
    Will fill your hearts with His perennial praise!

---

   * "Nothing tends more to promote health of body and of soul
than does a spirit of gratitude and praise. It is a positive duty to
resist melancholy, discontented thoughts and feelings—as much
as it is to pray."—*The Ministry of Healing*, p. 251.

Camp Meeting Time

Camp meeting time is a blessed time,
  A time when we may hear
A message from our Lord sublime,
  A time when God draws near.

Camp meeting is a special place
  Where fellowship is sweet,
And we are fortified by grace
  Beside the mercy seat.

A time and place to sing and pray,
  And hear the Spirit's voice;
A time and place to grow each day—
  A time we should rejoice!

The Pacific Union Conference Centennial
100 Years—100,000 Membership

We bring congratulations in this great centennial year
And pause to pay a tribute to each faithful pioneer.
They'd thrill to know your membership—one hundred thousand souls;
They would rejoice to see how you have reached so many goals!

What were the noble qualities their lives and labors show?
What was the spirit of the men who helped this work to grow!
Ah! They were men of vision and men of courage, too,
And they revealed these qualities in all they had to do!

The weekly *Signs* was founded in eighteen seventy-four,
The printed pages published became a treasure store.
The work was slow at first, and yet, foundations laid were
    strong,
For all those pioneers had learned to sing the victor's song.

> The Fresno church was built so large it served them sixty
>   years,
> But think of all the sacrifices of those pioneers!
> In nineteen four the Loma Linda dream was just a plan;
> The dream has now come true to cheer the heart of God
>   and man!

O think of ev'ry college, each academy, and school,
And think of all our churches built to teach the golden rule.
Consider ev'ry clinic and each sanitarium, too;
Each institution is a monument to God, it's true!

> With these and such an army of one hundred thousand
>   souls,
> Why not arise and quickly reach the highest of all goals—
> A finished work—it thrills our hearts to think what that
>   will mean,
> To walk the golden streets, at last, in heaven so serene!

Ah! No more sin or sorrow, and no more pain or tears,
And we'll rejoice together with those loyal pioneers!
And so we bring our tribute of respect and love and praise,
And place on ev'ry member our heartfelt verbal leis!

> Not only for the marvelous work that through the years
>   you've done,
> But for the finished work you'll do before the set of sun!

When Christmas Comes

The world grows old with care and stress and strife—
  Then Christmas comes,
  And battle drums
    Soon cease,
    And peace
  Smiles in the gate.
  Man's spiteful spate
Of hate gives way to love that sweetens life,
  And all men then
  Turn young again.

The world grows old with greed and doubt and fear—
  Then Christmas comes,
  And man succumbs
    To song,
    And wrong
  Begins to wane,
  And mad man's reign
Of sin gives way to faith and hope and cheer.
  The songs then sung
  Make men feel young.

Man's mind grows old and cold while grubbing *gold*—
  Then Christmas comes,
  And man's heart hums
    With mirth
    On earth.
  A Baby's birth
  Has changed man's worth!
  With such songs sung
  By ev'ry tongue,

The world turns young,
And love and faith unfold, to young and old,
The sweetest story ever told.
   And while we sing,
   The angels bring
   Life's sugar plums,
   When Christmas comes!

These miracles make life sublime!
Why not have Christmas all the time?

Dedicating the Table Rock Church

We've come this holy Sabbath day
And by the things we do and say
We formally will dedicate
Our precious church to God this date
   Of July 8 in sixty-seven.

We also consecrate our hearts
And seek the grace that God imparts,
That in this world of mortal strife
Each one of us will, through his life,
   Reveal the Christ, the Way to heav'n.

We love this church from floor to steeple,
But most important are the people.
And so we plead this solemn hour
To fill us with the Spirit's power.

May God's Shekinah glory shine
From church and us with light divine.

Our Vacation Bible School

Our VBS for sixty-seven
Brought us all much nearer Heaven.
Our hearts were thrilled; our souls were stirred
By all the wondrous things we heard.
The Bible was the theme this year
And brought us all much holy cheer.
We liked each story and each song
That taught us how to shun the wrong,
To love the right, the good, the true,
And honor God in all we do.
Our teachers all were sweet and kind
And helped each one improve his mind.
They kept us out of mischief, too,
By teaching us some things to do.
They showed us things to please our eyes;
Each day we had some fresh surprise.
They taught us crafts and manual arts,
And we made things that thrilled our hearts.
We built some church banks—made by hand.
We think they're finest in the land.
We'll keep our money in the banks
And give to God our hearty thanks,
For treasures greater far than wealth
Are happy hearts and mental health.
Another craft we learned one morn
Was little owls made out of corn.
We made mosaic trivets, too;
It's something anyone could do
With such teachers as we had.
These useful things pleased mom and dad.
And they were also pleased to see

How happy we had learned to be
And more obedient, too. Dad said,
It's lots more fun than "raising Ned."
Mom said that I had turned so good
And doing all the things I should.
Their hearts were really filled with cheer
I'd come to VBS this year.
We thank our teachers, bless their hearts—
They taught us love and manual arts!
Our VBS in sixty-seven
Has really brought us nearer Heaven.

The Challenge of the New Year

The holiday bells, with their voices of gold,
Ring in the new year as they ring out the old.
While ringing they're bringing a message so clear,
Inspiring new dreams, full of hope and great cheer.
These dreams can come true and success will be ours,
If we can remember, through life's fleeting hours,

To make the world brighter and better each day,
By smiling at people on life's weary way,
By lifting their load as they're limping along,
By sharing our faith or by singing a song,
By penning our poems inspiring fresh hope,
By helping solve problems with which men must cope.

By sweet'ning our motives, improving our arts,
By starting fresh fires in cold rooms and cold hearts.
By finding true values in Heaven's great plan,
By seeing the good in each frail fellow man.
By noting the beauty still flooding the earth,
And thanking the Lord for the things of real worth.

With joy face the future, let courage now rise,
With hope in our hearts and with smiles in our eyes.
With love in our labors and peace in our souls,
Our dreams can come true and we'll reach life's great goals!
With happy bells ringing the gospel of cheer,
We thrill with the challenge of this great new year!

A Happy New Year

A happy new year! Oh, what can it bring?
New love, new life, if we walk with the King!
New inspiration at the dawn of each day!
New wisdom the statutes of truth to obey.
New zeal to leap with the rising sun,
New joys at night when our work is all done.
New insight to plumb the depths of God's love—
New heights and new breadths and the fullness thereof!
New visions to see the great goals of life;
New courage to meet earth's stress and its strife.
New treasures to find if we really look;
New searchings for gems in the Blessed Book!
New patience to bear the burdens we face,
New peace to run our daily race.
New strength to help the ones who are down,
New fervor to claim our heavenly crown!
New pleasures that foster the smiling art—
New tonic of power for the human heart.
New loyalties for the blest brotherhood,
New rev'rence for church and things that are good.
New faith in the things that were prophesied,
New meekness when self becomes crucified.
New vict'ries gained when we've done our best,
New thrills to feel when we've stood life's test!

Where Was the Crown?

'Twas a blessed morn,
When Christ was born:
  A mother's sweet sigh,
  A Baby's low cry,

    And the heavens rang,
    As the angels sang

      Their soulful lays
      And paeans of praise,

Of infinite mysteries of Bethlehem!

Then shepherds came
To lisp His name,

  To worship Him
  In the twilight dim,

    In a manger stall,
    Not a palace tall.

      Did not angels sing
      Of the new-born King?

But where was His royal diadem?

When You make up Your jewels, Lord, we will be Thine,
  Pearls of great price—gems of renown—
What price have we paid for our pearl divine?
  Yet we are the gems for Thy royal crown!

Welcome to a Pastor

We welcome you to come and share
Our joys of worship, work, and prayer.
Lift up the Book, we love it so,
And tell us what we ought to know.
        Come and share!

We welcome you to come and view
The mighty work we have to do.
Show us the blueprint, show us how
To consummate our world work now!
        Come and see.

We welcome you to come and hear
The secret of a great career.
Vision and voice, Christ and His Word—
A vision seen, a clear voice heard!
        Come and hear!

We welcome you to come and pray
The very words that Christ did say,
And plead for wisdom, grace, and power
To meet the challenge of the hour.
        Come and pray!

We welcome you to come and seek
For precious souls, with tear-stained cheek,
The lost and dying—other sheep
For whom the loving Christ did weep.
        Come and seek!

We welcome you to come and share
The wealth to which we've been made heir.
And make this precious message known;
Christ soon will reign upon His throne!
       Go and tell!

We welcome you to come and do
The work that Christ has planned for you.
God calls! Accept, whate'er the loss,
This sweeping challenge of the cross!
       Come and do!

We welcome you with hand and heart,
And may God every day impart
His grace—and bless your family, too,
And all the work you have to do.
       We welcome you!

We pledge our loyalty and love—
God add His blessing from above!

Candle of Memories

(For a wedding service.)

Today you light a candle
   Of memories and dreams;
Each year you will relight it,
   Survey its golden gleams;
While rev'ling in its radiant glow,
   Rehearse life's sweetest themes!

Too many place their mem'ries
  In mem'ry's box with care;
The box becomes a casket,
  And dreams lie buried there.
Your plan is best, relight love's fires,
  And blessed mem'ries share!

Tonight your brilliant candle
  With flames of love and light
That shine on happy faces
  Is such a glorious sight;
It lightens up the future,
  To keep your pathway bright.

May all your anniversary days
Be beacon lights of love and praise
Along your path of peace and love,
To Father's royal home above!

Ordination

The hour has come to set apart
A man who loves the sacred art
Of preaching! Father, fill his heart
      This hour!
He needs Thy holy unction, Lord;
His life must be in full accord
With Thee, to preach the living Word
      With power!

Dear Father, fill his heart and mind
With love to make him always kind,
And zeal to go and seek and find
      More souls!
Give him fresh vision, anoint his eyes
For dawn's east window of divine surprise
Inspired to grasp the heav'nly prize—
      Life's goals!

God, keep him humble, touch his tongue
With flames of fire and keep him young,
To preach with power and healthy lung
      Thy truth!
God, bless him and his faithful wife
To rise above all earthly strife!
Ordain him as he gives his life
      And youth!

The Better Way

Satan trembles when he sees
A thankful Christian on his knees.
The only person Satan fears
Is one who ever perseveres
In serving God in all his ways
And daily sings his Father's praise.
This man has found a better way
And makes each dawn Thanksgiving Day.

Round the Globe

Congo Roads

These Congo roads I can't describe,
  There's no apt definition;
Though you indulge in diatribe,
  You drive with premonition.

You can't describe just what is what,
  Unless in desperation
You show exactly what it's not,
  By way of illustration.

They are not superhighways,
   And you will not find four lanes;
And though the scenery you may praise,
   You feel some aches and pains.

And when you drive o'er mountain trails
   That wind just like a snake
Your whole digestive system fails.
   You lose your meals, for travel's sake.

These roads were never paved with gold,
   With bricks, concrete, or tar,
And if the bitter truth were told,
   Not fit for any car.

Perhaps within the distant past
   Some grading had been done,
But when in mud hole you're stuck fast
   You're sure they missed this one.

And when roads turn to rivers wide
   And you can't see the shore
And you behold the rising tide
   That's coming through your door;

Your car-boat battles with the flood,
   You know the engine's wet,
And though the car grinds through the mud,
   You fear your sun has set.

But when you've covered all the miles,
   And friends help you unload,
Their welcome and their hearty smiles
   Eclipse the rigors of the road.

The Bells of Freedom

(Part of an address given in the National Stadium in Kingston, Jamaica, July 4, 1965.)

One hundred eighty-nine years ago,
The Liberty Bell was ringing, and, lo,
Its message of freedom was sent to the world,
And scores of new flags have been unfurl'd.

But political freedom is not enough,
Much more is needed, for the going is rough.
Spiritual freedom's the need of the hour,
Spiritual blessings, spiritual power.

Freedom from hate and freedom from tears,
Freedom from want and freedom from fears.
Freedom from worry, freedom from doubt,
Freedom from sin, within and without.

Freedom from sorrow, freedom from pain,
Freedom from troubles that drive men insane.
Freedom from sickness, freedom from death,
Freedom from taxes on all but your breath.

Freedom from heartaches, freedom from strife,
Freedom to live a beautiful life.
Freedom from suff'ring, freedom from wrong,
Freedom, dear freedom, 'tis man's sweetest song.

Physical freedom, we know it is great,
But how does spiritual freedom rate?
Many on earth are cowards today,
And shout, "Better Red than dead," they say.

But brave martyrs pray with their bated breath,
"God, give us freedom or give us death!"
The coming of Christ is the only plan
That guarantees freedom to ev'ry man.

Permanent freedom for all who believe,
Permanent freedom for all who receive;
Permanent freedom for body and mind,
Permanent freedom for all mankind.

Will you be ready to claim your prize,
When Christ in glory bursts from the skies?
Will you be ready to look in His face?
Are you *now* ready to stand in your place?

Here in this National Stadium today,
I urge every one to stand up and say,
"Jamaica for Christ!" O lift up your voice,
Let's cause all heav'n and earth to rejoice!

Our Rendezvous

(Written at Finland Junior College, Turku, Finland.)

We have a rendezvous with Christ,
However, it's not bargain priced;
    It will require all we are worth,
    To meet our destiny on earth.

And yet if we will pay the price
And gladly make the sacrifice,
    And if we truly stand the test
    Of all life's bargains, it is best!

For what we think is loss or pain
Will bring us everlasting gain.
  I'm glad that two and two make four,
  And what we sow will yield much more!

Tulip Time in Holland

In Holland springtime is tulip time!
Why shouldn't my heart burst forth in rhyme
Midst beautiful gardens so sublime
  As here by the Zuider Zee?
For tulip time is a happy time,
A beauty pageant in pantomime,
The choicest colors of any clime
  Are here for the world to see!

Salute these people so brave and so strong,
Who took their land from the sea—was that wrong?
And planted their flowers while singing a song,
  Here by this ancient sea.
They've made their country a garden fair,
A riot of color everywhere;
Where can you find such scenes to compare
  With these by the Zuider Zee?

They battled the flood and were satisfied
To claim the land as they fought the tide,
And won with justifiable pride
  By striving without surcease!
They conquered the sea with patient toil,
And made its wasteland earth's richest soil,
And gave to the world its precious spoil—
  Gardens of tulips and peace!

Make Room

"They laid him in a manger because there was no room in the inn." Luke 2:8.

(Written in Bangkok, Thailand.)

Make room in your mind
For Christ, if you'd find
　The joy He has promised His own.
Make room in your heart,
And Christ will impart
　His power as He rules on the throne.
Make room in your life
For Christ, then the strife
　And the gloom you have known will cease.
Make room in your soul,
For Christ is the goal
　Of the man who would find true peace!

On Leaving South Africa

(To H. W. Peterson, my traveling companion in Trans-Africa.)

What memories I fondly will cherish
　As I leave this enchanted land,
With its farms and majestic mountains,
　And its ocean's glittering strand.

This trip on South Africa's highways
　Was a source of endless delight,
With wonders piled upon wonders
　From morning till late in the night.

What wonderful flora and fauna,
　And the rarest of birds to sing.

With Hanepoort grapes, fit for angels,
   And apples, fit for a king.

The great ostrich farms of the desert
   And the grandeur of old Cape Town,
With Table Mount tow'ring above it,
   Which serves as a beautiful crown.

The marvelous Helderberg College,
   The view of the mountain and sea,
To look at those wonderful students
   Was a real inspiration to me.

We saw the fabulous Cango Caves,
   Among the greatest grottoes on earth,
And thrilled at the exquisite workmanship
   Of nature's art of infinite worth.

A night spent on Beacon Island
   With the surf gently lulling to sleep,
And the sight of the ships at daybreak,
   Going forth to fish in the deep.

We'd read the tales of Mossel Bay,
   And we found the "Post Office Tree,"
And the spring where da Gama and Diaz
   Filled their barrels for trips at sea.

They'd found the sea route to India
   And fabulous wealth of the East;
They bartered a bell with the Hottentots,
   For a big fat ox for a feast!

What beautiful modern cities,
    With parks to delight your eyes
And climate to rival any on earth,
    With the smile of these friendly skies.

The hotels have all been refurbished,
    To match an exclusive club.
You can bring your electric razor now
    And bathe in your private tub.

They're ready to welcome the tourist,
    With prices to please any Scot.
Their services match the best on earth!
    I'm frank to say, "This is the spot!"

Consider the wonderful game reserves,
    Where the eyes of man still can see
The wildlife of this great continent
    In their fantastic pageantry.

They live in their natural setting,
    In their tropical world they roam,
And we photograph their strange antics,
    Then take these wild animals home.

Soon elephants will stampede my parlor,
    And zebras will walk in my den.
Giraffes will gaze in our sun porch,
    And monkeys start using my pen.

But it's not just animals I'm taking back
    To become a part of my home and heart,

But the blessed memory of people,
　More than African works of art.

I'm taking home vivid impressions
　Of the work of the pioneers,
A work built on solid foundations
　That has stood the test of the years.

But I like the dreams of the future
　Much more than the tales of the past,
With dynamic programs like TABSA,
　We'll see a finished work at the last.

My trip now is nearly over,
　But I must see Victoria Falls;
And I must see Solusi Mission
　Before the Good Captain calls.

How blest are my eyes for what they've seen
　And my ears for what they have heard.
How happy my heart as I've seen the saints
　Respond to the call of the living Word!

What wonderful traveling companions,
　What blessed fellowship and sweet;
And the rich experiences of every day
　Made our cup of joy complete.

But now I must say a fond farewell
　And thank you for love you have given,
And pray God to richly reward you
　In the final reckoning in heaven.

A World on Fire

(Written in Cardiff, Wales.)

A world gone mad—a world aflame
With hate and doubt and moral shame.
The minds of men are full of fear
Of what is taking place this year.

Man drifts upon a stormy sea,
And helpless as mere man can be
Without a compass or a chart,
Without a pilot's hand or heart.

Philosophy has failed to find
A way of hope and peace of mind;
And atheism brought its curse,
While politics has made things worse.

The world of finance, it is sure,
Has not helped make mankind secure.
Technology has brought no hope—
With Frankensteins of death we cope!

    With Christ we have an endless hope, my friend,
    But without Christ we have a hopeless end!

My Heart Leaps Up

Man's Desire for Immortality

Each person on earth desires to live long,
  And no one wants to grow old.
It helps to stay young if we sing a song
  While the sunset is turning to gold.

Life's Rising Tide

There is a tide, as Shakespeare said,
Which, if we wisely use,
Will lift us to new heights ahead—
We're lost if we refuse!

Dedications

We dedicate our churches
    For their high and holy task.
Why not dedicate our Christian homes?
    Is a question I would ask.

What plans we make for churches
    As we lay each cornerstone!
Invite the city fathers,
    And what speeches they intone!

And when we dedicate the church
    What fanfare and all such!
But we avoid all this for homes—
    Don't they amount to much?

Now really, are we thinking straight
    To treat our homes this way?
For they're the real foundation
    Of society, I'd say.

So why not dedicate each home,
    And build on holy ground;
And make each home a hallowed place
    Where love and peace are found.

What God Has Done for Me

"Tell those whom you visit . . . how blessed you have been."—
Christian Service, p. 124.

My God has been so good to me
To make the mountains and the sea,
To give us sunshine and the rain,
Producing fields of golden grain.

God made the peacock's tail and wing,
And gave the birds their power to sing.
He put the colors in the flowers
And blesses all life's fleeting hours.

My God has been so good to me,
Forgave my sins and set me free.
I'm free to eat the best of food,
And do those things which God calls good.

I've found the cross is Christ's plus sign.
It adds life's best in God's design.
The noblest, purest, truest, too,
Enriching everything we do!

It's positive, gives me life's best,
The things I need to stand life's test.
It only takes away from me
Those things that spoil man's destiny!

God gives good books and music fine
And purest joys that are divine.
God gives such peace that my heart sings,
I find such joy in simple things.

And then to add to all of this,
God promises eternal bliss.
But were no heav'n beyond earth's strife,
I've had earth's best in this brief life!

All this my God has done for me,
I wish all men could be as free.
Yes, freed from habits that defile,
By hope that helps the heart to smile!

A Thank-you Card

We thank you, dear friends,
For a gift that ne'er ends,
For a friendship that grows
Like a beautiful rose;
For a rich tasty meal,
With a flavor appeal.
The food was "delish"—
Indeed, ev'ry dish
Was a "gourmet's delight"
With the food cooked just right,
With such lovely décor,
Could one ask for more?
Along with such food,
What sweet brotherhood!
We're glad we hang, see,
On your friendship tree!
May we, bye and bye,
Build our home close by?

The Gift of Friendship

A friend is someone who knows you—
 Not merely knows your name
But knows your faults, yet still true blue
 He loves you just the same.

Ah! friendship is a precious gift,
 When each one loves the other;
A true friend always brings a lift—
 He's better than a brother!

Is loyalty the greatest trait
 Within the human heart?
Is this what makes a friendship great,
 With such power to impart?

Ah! love waits not till friends are dead,
 Or friendship crashes on the rocks;
Instead, kind, fragrant words are said—
 We break our alabaster box!

Homeward Bound

This morning as I fly
 With modern wings,
Up in the azure sky,
 My glad heart sings
A sweet and happy song,
 A joyful sound.
My jet plane won't take long—
 I'm homeward bound!

8

A Successful Marriage

A successful marriage, they say, requires
     Falling in love many times.
But who is the person your heart desires?
     To whom do you write your rhymes?

The same person, always, every time?
Ah! this will help to make life sublime!

Another Great Congress

This congress has been wonderful,
     We came with great desire;
And God has granted our request—
     Filled us with holy fire.

We have such precious fellowship,
     As love and joy increase
We're thankful for these blessings—
     God fills our hearts with peace.

We're glad for all these meetings—
     The leaders have our thanks,
For at this laymen's congress
     They've put "tigers in our tanks."

Peace and Harmony

As peace is wise man's masterpiece of reason,
     So harmony will triumph over wrong!
When music reigns as queen to banish treason,
     The heart of man will sing its sweetest song!

In Broader Perspective

"Treasures, Trinkets, and Trash"

(Dedicated to Sherman Clark, whose career in promotion of missionary periodicals was an inspiration.)

This sign hung over an antique shop,
"Treasures, Trinkets, and Trash."
It caught the eye of each passerby,
Reacting on him in a flash.

Some spend their lives on trinkets, some trash,
    And some seek treasures of art.
The human race in life's swift pace
    Pursues the goal of the heart.

For what am I spending my silver and gold?
    For what am I giving my time?
In earth's mad strife, am I spending my life
    On trash, or on treasure sublime?

Vision and Character

"Which the vulture's eye has not seen." Job 28:7.

The vulture, as he's poised for flight,
Upon yon mountain's dizzy height,
    Sees not Tut's tomb or treasure store,
    He looks for dead things, nothing more.
In yonder dusty caravan
There is an earnest, noble man,
    Lord Carnarvon, he'll risk his health,
    To find King Tutankhamen's wealth!

APPETITE THE BASIS OF CHARACTER

The vulture looks for carrion,
And at the break of ev'ry dawn
    He sees with telescopic sight
    The carcasses left by the night.
He sees not Tutankhamen's tomb,
Or treasures in the mountain's gloom.
    His appetite, 'tis plain to view,
    Makes him a vulture, through and through.

Man looks for things both rich and rare,
And searches for them everywhere.
    He has no telescopic eyes,
    But seeks for rare things till he dies.

Man's character—now, please friend, hark—
Is what that man does in the dark!
    What's his desire? Try this prime quiz,
    For what man wants tells what man is!

CHARACTER THE BASIS OF VISION

What appeals to the vulture's sight?
What appeals to his appetite!
    Because a man's a man, that's right,
    He sees things precious in his sight.

Two men looked out through prison bars,
One saw the mud, one saw the stars!
    Man found Tut's tomb and treasure chest,
    The vulture's keen sight missed the best!

VISION THE BASIS OF ACHIEVEMENT

Man does not want or see or get
The carcass, yet has no regret.
    The vulture has no appetite
    For precious gems hid from his sight.

He does not see and does not find
The things that tantalize mankind.
    Man's vision seeks and finds the best,
    Pursuing his eternal quest!

Television

Television is a mighty educational power;
It is, perhaps, earth's most effective teacher at this hour,
The greatest educational force invented yet by man.
How tragic Satan uses it in his nefarious plan!
That's why we must have safeguards and discriminating
      sense
To shut out each debasing program in our self-defense.

Unless you have this strength of will and courage to say No,
TV converts your home into a modern burlesque show;
It turns the sanctity of home into a gambling den,
A wrestling match, or night club, with its scenes debauching
      men.
It glorifies the questionable, the shady things of life,
And often makes a farce of home, the husband, and the wife.

Some little children sit for hours before a TV set.
How much do they remember and how much can they
      forget?
Before their eyes and plastic minds what orgies are por-
      trayed?
What murders, crimes, and robberies and mystery plots are
      laid?
Those children sit there spellbound; sometimes petrified
      with fear,
Or punctuate a Wild West murder with a lusty cheer.

You say you like to prove all things and hold fast what is
      good?
But do you really do it in the way you know you should?
How dare you spend your precious time in Satan's garbage
      can,

Reviewing all the filth to find some mental food for man?
I know a better source of food to feed your mind and heart—
The timeless, priceless treasure that the gifts of God impart!

What captures your imagination soon will capture you,
So flee the fierce hypnotic spell of Satan's rendezvous.
Refuse to hear the siren song, unmask the devil's grin,
Unveil the vile and hideous serpent charming you to sin.
Determine you will only see and hear what things are pure,
For by beholding we are changed—our destiny is sure!

Ezekiel's Vision

Ezekiel saw a vision of God's sapphire-studded throne;
Above it was a rainbow with a glory all its own.
He saw a wheel within a wheel, he saw a mighty hand;
He saw so many symbols that he could not understand.
He saw the lightning flashing, he saw God's glory shine,
But in it all was order and a harmony divine.
While gazing on this vision he felt his utter need
And humbly bowed in worship before such power and
    speed.

  Ezekiel heard the voice of God, he knew that he was
      called;
  At once went into action—did not merely stand en-
      thralled.
  He went to meet the people with a message to impart,
  And all the while the fire of God was burning in his heart.
  He said he "sat where they sat" so the people's needs he
      knew;
  He showed them love and sympathy in all he had to do.

The people still were stubborn—with what problems he
    did cope!
But patiently he carried on and talked of God and hope.

Ezekiel felt the hand of God upon him all the time;
He knew that he was called of God to do His work sublime.
Ezekiel saw the vision to fit him for his work,
And from that sacred moment, no duty did he shirk.
God called him to a mountaintop the vision to renew,
And gave explicit counsel of things he had to do.
May God renew our vision as He did with that great man,
And help us find the power and speed to fulfill Heaven's
    plan!

The Measure of Success

"The measure of success is not whether you have a tough problem to deal with, but whether it's the same problem you had last
year."—JOHN FOSTER DULLES.

    The measure of success in each life's case
        Is not how tough the problem that you fear,
    But can it be the problem that you face
        Is just the same as that you faced last year?

Undermining the Pillars

The person who would try to undermine
The strong foundations of our hope divine,
    Is tearing down supports which, in God's plan,
    Sustain the faith and courage of each man.

Eloquence

The art of eloquence, somewhere I've heard,
Is this: To know when not to say a word!

SECTION 13

Smile Awhile

"Christians Sing Hymns and Pay Taxes"

When Pliny wrote the emperor,
  According to his view,
The Christians he described, it seems,
  Were honest, glad, and true.
He wrote: "These Christians sing their hymns
  And pay their taxes, too."

Do we sing hymns at tax time?
  Come now! What do we do?

Canada's Prime Minister Hospitalized

When Pearson, the man,
Was rushed to the san,
They found him mad as a hatter;
Since he was so serious,
And yet not delirious,
They wondered what was the matter!

He's not one to faint
With ev'ry complaint,
He's not a proverbial crabber;
Though body and brain
Were racked with his pain,
The cause he assigned—"De Gaulle Blabber!"

Alternatives

'Tis said that after forty-five our exercise depends
On *jumping at conclusions* and *running down* our friends.
While some may be contented to merely *pass the buck,*
And others seem so satisfied to simply *push their luck,*
Yet some are very quick to *dodge* each hard and hateful task;
They *jog* right by! You know, some day I'd really like to ask,
Why is it that these folks can only exercise their knees
When they can *side-step* all of life's responsibilities!
Some act as if just *standing up* and then just *sitting down*
Could somehow, in the end of time, earn them the victor's
     crown.
In fact, for some, the toughest task, it seems, at any age,
Is just to learn to *draw their breath* and then to *draw their
     wage.*

His Problem

"I have a problem, doctor," the patient patient said,
    And counted off his symptoms one by one.
"It's very serious, doctor, and it's something that I dread,
    At times I can't remember what I've done."

The doctor listened patiently unto the bitter end,
    Then posed this simple question as routine,
"About how long now, would you say you've had this
        problem, friend?"
    "What problem, doc? What problem do you mean?"

"Big Wheels"

So many people on this earth
Are very proud about their worth;
Inflated like a big balloon,
And strutting like a vain baboon.
They're everywhere—you need not search—
You'll find them in the world or church.
Puffed up with pride, sometimes a pin
Can burst their bubble with a din.
Yes, ev'ry group has these "big wheels,"
And each one tells you how he feels
On any subject you can name.
The way he rants on is a shame.
And I have learned through passing years
This simple fact, with aching ears:

The longer "the spoke" ("big wheel" kind),
The greater is "the tire," I find.

Signs of Old Age

There are three certain signs which clearly show
Advancing age—approaching life's December.
The first is loss of memory—and would you know—
The other two, just now, I can't remember!

Dedicated to Dr. Edward L. R. Elson

(Pastor of Dwight Eisenhower's church while he was President.)

A preacher named Elson, it seems,
Was moved by high vision and dreams,
   And people who heard him
   Knew something had stirred him
With great theological themes!

Bad Poems vs. Bad Checks

A banker may write a bad poem,
   And all that we do is to smile;
But poets who dare to write a bad check,
   May sit in the hoosegow awhile.

The Fate of the Poet Laureate

"Our poet laureate" I'm called,
And you might think I'd be enthralled;
   Instead, I feel alarmed about my fate.
I've heard about an alligator,
Named Laurie by a commentator.
   I ask, am I the poet Laurie ate?

Index

Date Due